SELF-ISH
is the new
SELFLESS

SELF-ISH
is the new
SELFLESS

Your pocketbook guide to feeling GOOD
without all the GUILT!

B. HANNAH

SELF-ISH is the new SELFLESS: Your pocketbook
guide to feeling GOOD without all the GUILT!

© 2020 B. Hannah

ISBN 13: 9798687723459

DESCRIPTION

Welcome to your Pocketbook Guide to start the path of living your most fulfilling life. Incorporate more *feel-good* days without the GUILT in this journey of replacing selfless acts with the positivity and necessity of being SELF-ISH! What was *once* considered a societal negative- toned word, *selfish*, has since been renewed with this author's remarkable perspective of breaking down the word into two distinct parts: *self* and *-ish*. The takeaway here is- we cannot be our best for others unless we are our best for ourselves. Covering talking points of self-care, communicating with purpose, navigating relationships, and prioritizing your needs. Don't be selfless and focus on others... be SELF-ISH and focus on yourself, how you spend your time alone, and how and when you will spend your time with others. **After all... haven't you heard? Self-ish is the new selfless!**

Throughout this guide, you can find the following short but sweet reads that consist of 3 sections: *The Pocketbook Guides*, *The Heartfuls*, and *The Random Stuff*. Readers are encouraged to embrace putting themselves first.

The Pocketbook Guides are focused on deciding who you want to be a part of your life and how. With an emphasis on choice, communication, and maintaining boundaries.

The Heartfuls encompass compassion and empathy

towards ourselves and others. The Heartfuls enhance mental health well-being through self-care, self-love, and a special focus on self-worth when seeking a life-long partner.

The Random Stuff is a hodgepodge focus of:
– Friendly reminders to keep ourselves healthy
– Reminders to do what we love most
– How to support "young ones" in recognizing and developing a passion
– A discussion of "college or no college" and preparing for a job interview

Making time to do things you enjoy and are interested in (even alone-embrace it) is what promotes a feel-good-more-often kind of life. A life that everyone deserves.

This book represents embracing the self with self-care, self-love, self-compassion, and SELF-ISH decisions.

Remember, we can't be our best for others if we are not our best for ourselves.

After all, didn't you hear? SELF-ISH is the new SELFLESS!

INTRODUCTION

You're probably thinking 'self-ish is the new selfless' sounds pretty selfish huh?

Let's break down the definition of selfish courtesy of Webster's dictionary and the definition of selfless courtesy of the Oxford dictionary.

As you'll see, society's perception of selfish rings true with Webster's dictionary definition. Just as Oxford's definition of selfless rings true with our society's perception. Take a look at the definitions below. I promise... the technicalities in this book will be short. I just want to make a point. A damn good point. Bear with me. And KEEP reading. Alright. Here we go.

Webster's definition of selfish:

Selfish—adjective

Collegiate definition 1: Concerned excessively or exclusively with oneself: seeking advantage, pleasure, or well-being without regard for others.

Collegiate definition 2: arising from concern with one's own welfare or advantage in disregard of others.

Hmm.... Wow. Sounds about right. That's pretty much how I grew up viewing the word selfish.

Oxford definition of selfless:

Selfless—adjective

Concerned more with the needs and wishes of others than with one's own.

Hmm… correct. Or in other words, what society subconsciously wants us to be. This is where the guilt comes in. Society pushes us to think being selfish is wrong and being selfless is the expectation.

Now. Let's look at the interpretation of why I say *self-ish* is the new selfless.

Look at the definition of self and the definition of *ish* separately.

Webster's definition of *self*:

Self—noun

Entry 2: the union of elements (such as body, emotions, thoughts, and sensations) that constitute the individuality and identity of a person.

Webster's definition of -ish:

"ish—adjective, suffix

Collegiate definition 1: of, relating to, or being.

If we look at the definitions of each of these

independently and then bring them together there is a whole new meaning of selfish. A positive meaning. The takeaway here for me is a meaning that encourages us to relate to being aware of how our body feels, being aware of our emotions, and being aware of our thoughts with purpose.

Doesn't that sound more fitting for healthier and more joy-filled moments? I think so, too. Who wants in? My hand is raised. I hope yours is too… as fast as the cast in The Breakfast Club when Assistant Principal Vernon asks if anyone needs to use the lavatory (great movie by the way). Speaking of The Breakfast Club, I've always admired this meaningful quote from the movie: "You see us as you want to see us. In the simplest terms, in the most convenient definitions." Let that sink in.

"We're all on team human here, and let's be honest-it's not an easy team to be on. It's stressful and taxing and worrisome, but it's also fulfilling and beautiful and bright." – Kristen Bell

PREFACE

A thought to live our lives by:

We cannot be our best for others unless we are our best for ourselves.

Read that again. And again.

The meaning?

Simply, if we do not take care of ourselves first, if we are not feeling our best—how can we be present, motivated, interested, and invested in the other parts of our lives?

We can't. And when we can't be fully present for others, we can feel tired, guilty, irritable, let down and defeated. And whatever else comes to mind you might be thinking and feeling.

It is vital to give ourselves permission to take care of ourselves. First.

Before our family, before our partners, before our kids, before our parents, before our workplace, before our RSVP obligations (that we probably changed our minds about). Think that sounds selfish? Think of this... wouldn't it be more traditionally "selfish" to show up annoyed, aggravated, distant, fatigued, passive aggressive, negative, and irritable? Making others around us feel the backlash of both our conscious and unconscious states of *being tired, feeling drained, and our negativity.* Choose you first. Put your needs first to be your best for others. I'm telling you, *self-ish* is the NEW selfless. Why? Because we cannot be our best for others unless we are our best for ourselves.

Every day we should be working to satisfy our basic needs and prioritize our leisure wants. I'm sharing a breakdown of why it is a survival skill to identify our basic needs and leisure wants—while learning how to be realistic and not overset—that can contribute to more feel-good days.

Feel-good days are key. Because reality is ups and downs. And sometimes there seem to be more downs. Looking forward to wants and needs is essential to gain and plan for more feel-good days.

The Pocketbook Guides

- Pocketbook Guide #1: Choosing words with confidence and communicating with purpose
- Pocketbook Guide #2: Choosing who deserves to know The Good, The Bad and The Ugly
- Pocketbook Guide #3: Deciding what you want more of and less of in your life
- Pocketbook Guide #4: Being aware of and enjoying the present
- Pocketbook Guide #5: Getting comfortable spending time with yourself

The Heartfuls

- Heartful #1: Mental health (What it is, How to support your own mental well-being)
- Heartful #2: How to support our loved ones
- Heartful #3: Why do people feel depressed if nothing bad has happened?
- Heartful #4: BE SELF-ISH when seeking a long-term partner

The Random Stuff

- Integrating peace and calm into your life using the 5 senses
- Necessary and important reminders for self-care
- Have a Bucket List
- Generating passion and meaning within children to promote a peaceful life

- College versus no College
- Applying for a job and attending an interview
- Activity List to promote joy, patience, and more feel-good moments in this life we live

By the end of this book my hope is you will be hearing recording artist Lizzo's song, Feeling Good As Hell, ringing in your ears.

THE
POCKETBOOK
GUIDES

Webster's definition of pocketbook:

Pocketbook—noun

Collegiate Definition (Entry 1 of 2): a small especially paperback book that can be carried in the pocket

Webster's definition of guide:

Guide—noun

Collegiate Definition (Entry 1 of 2) 1c: something that provides a person with guiding information (intransitive verb): to act or work as a guide

Pocketbook Guide #1: Choosing words with confidence and communicating with purpose

Why choose words with confidence, you ask? Being more precise at explaining our requests and choices allows us to be comfortable with those choices and encourages us to follow through.

Communicating with purpose has a lot to do with being aware of yourself and choosing to be aware of others around you.

Before communicating your requests and expectations for yourself you need to be able to identify who you want to share your thoughts with and why. What is your hopeful purpose of sharing your thoughts, expectations, concerns and desires with this person or persons.

When considering others, have expectations of how they may respond or react through their words and behavior. Prepare yourself for their possible responses and consider how you may react to their response (based on past interactions) and how you will want to respond to them in return. Then choose and commit to yourself, ahead of time, how you intend to react.

There's definitely a difference between how you will likely react and how you want to react. You can even practice your reaction. Putting it to practice can consist of envisioning the scenarios in your mind or talking about them with a person you trust (maybe a friend, or a therapist- just sayin').

Consider what it is you want to share and why.

Here are some examples:

- Maybe you want to share with someone how much you appreciate them. Take the time to identify why this is important for you to share with them and share that. Continue the conversation by explaining how their actions, company, support or love for you makes you feel.
- Maybe you want to share with someone that you admire them.
- Maybe you want to share with someone that you are angry, sad, hurt or all of these feelings.

Consider when and where the most appropriate time may be to share your thoughts. But before doing so ask the person if they would be okay to listen to you share your thoughts. Perhaps allow that person to choose times they are willing to set aside and choose from that list what best aligns with your availability. By asking for permission, you are inviting them to be a part of the conversation at a time that is best for the both of you.

What are ways you would like to practice your communication style?

_____

_____

_____

_____

_____

_____

_____

_____

_____

_____

_____

_____

Pocketbook Guide #2: Choosing who deserves to know The GOOD, The BAD and The UGLY

I want to dramatically say with emphasis this is soooooooooooooo important. You've heard the saying, forgive and forget?

"F" that. Seriously.

You can forgive if you choose but there is no forgetting. That's like telling someone who just lost a loved one, "Time heals all wounds." Yeaaaaaah, followed by an exaggerated mmhmm. And you know what else? I'm here to tell you, you don't have to forgive either. Don't fall into that tug-of-war of conflicted feelings dictated by societal norms and self-doubt. We feel the way we do for a reason. We do not have to forget to gain a sense of peace or to move forward. Peace comes with choosing how you will interact with that person going forward. Peace comes with making the best set of decisions for yourself. You choose.

You choose if you want to avoid being in their presence. You choose if you want to tell them to respect your choice of not wanting them in all parts of your life. You choose if you want to share with them why you have chosen distance. You choose what you want to share with them and anyone who challenges you or asks you for an explanation. You choose who you think deserves to be a part of your life. You choose who you feel deserves to know what you're going through in your life. You choose who you want to share your decision-making process with.

Consider who is supportive and who is not. Consider making decisions about what we share with others based on how those individuals make us feel. Allow yourself as much time as needed to make your decisions about who, when, and how someone will be in your life. And the best part about this? You can change your mind at any time.

Who do you feel supported by and how?

_____

_____

_____

_____

_____

_____

_____

_____

_____

_____

_____

_____

Pocketbook Guide #3: How to decide what you want more of and less of in your life

This is harder than one would think. This has to be thought about with some serious self-awareness and self-reflection.

Let's start with people. It means so much to take time to identify who you truly look forward to spending time with and why. Is this person a friend, a neighbor, a family member, a co-worker? Identify the reasons you enjoy spending time with them. How do these special people make you feel when you spend time with them? Maybe you laugh, you may have a safe place to cry, or you may feel listened to. And how do they make you feel about yourself? Do you feel at ease? Maybe comfortable or relaxed? Where and how do you usually spend time with these people? By identifying why you enjoy spending time with them you can then consider how often you see them, and choose to make more time to see them.

Think about places and things. Be thoughtful in your selection. Where do you feel most comfortable spending time with this person: in their home or yours? Enjoying a cup of coffee together talking about life, family, future plans? Enjoying a good meal together at your favorite restaurant or cooking a meal together? Maybe you have a movie night and process the film afterwards. Ask yourself what do I love about spending time with this person? Why do I feel good when I spend time with this person? When can I make time to spend with this person?

Choose timeframes and places that are realistic. If you have kids consider their age and where they will be when you are in the company of other people. Do you want a quiet place to spend time with one another? What time of day (and day of week) will this be the most achievable? If you have children, roommates, family or a partner around one should expect interruptions and distraction. But have a plan ahead of time. Discuss with them expectations of your scheduled get together and how you hope to have them respect your time. Commit to a plan on how you are going to tame any distractions—and give yourself permission to follow through—to ensure you are able to enjoy your planned get together.

What do you want more of in your life?

_____

_____

_____

_____

_____

_____

_____

_____

_____

_____

_____

_____

Pocketbook Guide #4: Being aware of and enjoying the present

Joys of life come from looking forward to future encounters with people, time to ourselves, and embracing the "feel goods" of the present. Consider the stuff you look forward to. Small things. Small things considering what you enjoy depending on the season, time of year and the time of day. Do not get caught up in thinking "big things" like vacations, travel, giving or receiving presents etc. are roads to happiness. That stuff is fun, even exciting to look forward to but at the end of the day it's the in-between stuff we experience the majority of the time. It is imperative we use our regular day to day time in a meaningful, thoughtful way to promote more 'feel goods.'

Here are some 'feel good' considerations:

- Maybe you want to make time to watch a television series you're interested in
- Make time to try a new recipe you've been interested in trying
- Maybe you've been considering starting or joining a book club
- Perhaps you would enjoy a monthly movie
- Perhaps you would enjoy a monthly movie night with your favorite snacks
- If you've been wanting to get a massage save up and schedule a service

What are your feel goods?

_____

_____

_____

_____

_____

_____

Not to sound like a broken record but after you identify yours don't forget-

- Choose who you want to be a part of your experience. Ask yourself "who deserves to be a part of this?"
- Make time to do the things you love. Don't rush the things you love.
- Don't be selfless and focus on others. Be SELF-ISH and focus on
- yourself, how you spend your time alone, and with others. After all, haven't you heard? Self-ish is the new selfless!

Pocketbook guide #5: Getting comfortable spending time with yourself

Alone time. Quiet time. Being comfortable being alone. There is so much stuff that comes from being alone; from how we spend our time alone.

Quiet alone time allows us to process experiences that continue to affect us (both positive and not). This allows us to be aware of our feelings which, in turn, can help us define how we feel and plan how we want to respond, in both the short term and the long term.

Alone time allows us quality time with ourselves. Think of a place you can comfortably sit back in silence, stare out or close your eyes, and just think. Quietly. Silence is golden, my friend.

On the flip side, here are different ways to spend alone time when you do not want to be caught up in your thoughts:

- Maybe you can just kick back on the couch in your comfy sweats and scroll through social media with music in the background.
- Maybe you have the opportunity to binge-watch your favorite TV show or series.
- Maybe you can finally soak in that hot bath with scented bubbles and a glass of wine or cup of tea.
- Or maybe you can get sucked back into your

book without interruption.

No matter how you spend it, alone time is a grand and worthy re-charge that is necessary to breathe and live healthy.

How do you hope to spend your alone time?

_____

_____

_____

_____

_____

_____

_____

_____

_____

_____

_____

_____

_____

THE HEARTFULS

Webster's definition of heartful:

Heartful—adjective: full of heartfelt emotion: hearty

"What's to be ashamed of? I went through a really rough time. And I'm quite proud that I got out of that."
– J.K. Rowling

Here you will find an eclectic bunch of heartfuls to enhance emotional well-being, and empowerment of choice that lead to more moments of peace.

Heartfuls 1-4 focus on mental health; ours and those of our loved ones.

But first, I'd like to talk about the benefits of therapy. As a therapist, I take any chance I get to discuss the value of joining therapy. You will read a plethora of useful information that discusses what therapy is, what mental well-being means, guidance for the self, and how to support loved ones in a time of need.

Therapy is a person you have chosen to dedicate a scheduled amount of your time to talk with about your life; to discuss experiences that come with feelings, concerns, hopes, ups, downs, confusing and conflicted thoughts, purpose and goals. Therapy can also be helpful to learn how to be a support to a loved one who may be suffering challenges in their own mental health. Therapy is special and unique; a one of a kind worthwhile experience.

***

For a moment I'd like to be light-minded here and share a playful example. SO. How does talking with a therapist REALLY differ from talking with a family member or friend?

... I must warn... profanity used in this example... take with a grain of salt!

– If you tell your best friend a story about why you hate your mother in law, followed by she's a real, BIG, B-I-T-C-H, your best friend might say "OMG what a B! I'd feel the same way."

– If you tell your therapist that you hate your mother in law because she's a B-I-T-C-H your therapist might respond "I hear you say that your mother in law is a B-I-T-C-H. Tell me about your mother in law and both your and your partner's relationship with her."

See the difference? Talking with your friend may encourage your current feelings. Talking with a therapist allows you to explore your thoughts and discuss how you may want to interact with your mother in law going forward. Told ya it's different.

On a serious note though, for a professional in-depth breakdown of how it's different- you will soon read in Heartful #1.

***

Alright, now back to discussing the benefits of therapy.

Therapy doesn't always feel good. It may even feel uncomfortable. Then why go, you ask? Feeling uncomfortable means change is in the works. Analogy anyone? If you've ever worked out for the first time in a long time, or maybe pushed yourself harder during a routine exercise, did you notice how your body hurts more? It can be uncomfortable. It might even suck for the time-being but you have set in motion both a mental and physical change. And the long-term outcome may be more satisfaction or contentment.

Sometimes, in therapy, you end up talking about things you never intended to. If your therapist brings up something that you are unsure you want to discuss, express that. One does not necessarily have to talk about what happened to better understand and work through uncomfortable stuff to have change. If a therapist asks you a question or makes a comment that perplexes you or makes you uncomfortable, tell them about it! Ask the therapist for the relevance of certain topics of discussion even if you expected them to come up. Sometimes you will be caught off guard by where the discussion takes you but it can be remarkable.

"The tragedy is not so much the experience that you're having. The tragedy is that we don't take the time to understand the meaning of it." – Robin Roberts

Remember... you can talk about feelings and thoughts without sharing minute details. Be open with your therapist. Their job is not to tell you what to do or give advice unless it's regarding your well-being (i.e. safety concerns, medication management, and medical concerns). The therapist is there to listen, reflect back what they hear, and foster exploration in your thoughts and feelings and how they align with where you want to be. But you have control to decide what your focus is within your therapeutic journey. The therapist may be steering the wheel to keep you on course but you have control of the brake. When you come to a stop, take a breath and share what's going on for you in that moment. Your thoughts, feelings, worries, concerns, maybe relief. Discuss it. This is your time. After all... didn't you hear? Self-ish is the new selfless.

Suggestions for finding the right fit when choosing a therapist:

If you have access to the internet consider doing an online search. PsychologyToday.com, has a national database where you can filter your search for a therapist by selecting the gender if you have a preference, the issues you hope to explore, location, fees, and type of insurance the therapist may take if you intend on using your health insurance coverage.

Read online profiles to determine the therapist's specialties and therapy models they incorporate into a therapeutic experience. Psychology Today allows the therapist to write a bit about their areas of focus and even post a video introducing themselves. Allow yourself to consider the following about who you think may be a good fit for you- who do you sense a connection with, after reading their profiles? Who might you feel the most comfortable with and why? What stands out to you? Their gender, the age you perceive them to be, or how long they have been practicing their profession? Their listed areas of expertise? Once you determine the therapists that you are considering, reach out to them to schedule a phone consultation. This allows you to get a feel for your connection through the phone. Have a list of questions ahead of time. Please, whatever you do, don't consider a therapist who is older ONLY because you think they have more life experience. Therapy is not based on one's life experience.

Therapy is a skillful conversation guided by research, therapeutic techniques and a client's self-report. After taking these steps, choose the therapist you felt the best connection with.

Other thoughts to consider: You may have heard of the following types of therapist: psychotherapist, psychologist, mental health counselor, professional counselor, social worker. We all have different education and areas of focus. If you are seeking a legitimate breakdown of the differences you can do an internet search of the descriptions of each profession within the state you reside. Every state has its own description and its own education for each of the aforementioned professions (which can vary in their titles state to state). So when you do your research make sure you are reading your information from a legitimate website (i.e. an office of professions government website). On the other hand, a psychiatrist and psychiatric nurse practitioner may offer some counsel however, their main focus is to discuss medication treatment options and prescribe medications to assist in the treatment of mental health conditions.

When it comes to cost: If you have health insurance that you intend to use you will want to contact your health insurance company to ask them if you have covered mental health services. If the answer is yes be sure to ask if you have a deductible that needs to be met before your co-pay kicks in. You will need to confirm with the therapist of interest if they accept your insurance. If you do not have health insurance and have to pay yourself or what is referred to as "out of pocket" or seeing an "out of network" (OON) provider, please know therapy is not always long term. Some people find after a handful of sessions they have gained enough self-awareness and self-accountability to put it into practice in the absence of therapy.

"It's okay to not be okay."
– Michael Phelps

"We would never tell someone with a broken leg that they should get it together. We don't consider taking medication for an ear infection something to be ashamed of. We shouldn't treat mental health conditions any differently."
– Michelle Obama

Heartful #1: Mental health well-being

What is mental health well-being? To put it plainly-how our mind and body feel causes us to experience a variety of thoughts and feelings. It is up to us to monitor when we feel good and when we desire to feel better. We determine what we want more of and less of in our lives. By identifying our feel-good moments followed by intentionally making time to experience these more often we can then start the path of well-being. Well-being is taking care of our thoughts and feelings by responding with a thoughtful and meaningful choice. Taking time to understand why we think, feel and act as we do permits us to live meaningful healthier lives. That segues into our Q&A.

Below are thoughtful and common 'Questions (Q) and Answers'

Q: Is there a difference between counseling and therapy?

Most often we hear the words counseling and therapy used interchangeably, both from those who are attending sessions and mental health professionals. Counseling may be viewed as providing guidance and education about symptoms, diagnoses, and prognosis. Therapy may be viewed as exploration of our thoughts, feelings and behaviors through skillful discussion prompted by the therapist. Most often, a bit of both will occur which can explain why the words are used interchangeably. It is worth the reminder that mental health credentials vary from state to state, which could also influence the language used.

Q: What can counseling and therapy be useful for?

One of my favorite questions. Everything. Therapy is good for the soul, good for self-challenge, and good for creating a path to work towards long term mental well-being. There are so many worthwhile reasons to join therapy. Here are a few examples:

- If you or others have noticed you do not enjoy activities or hobbies as you used to. If you have uncertainty making decisions.
- If you feel overwhelmed or underwhelmed with life, work, a partner, your children or family members. If you have interest in practicing different ways to communicate.
- If you have interest in managing emotions that come with a medical condition, mental health condition or addiction, or if you have a loved one who is working to manage their own mental health or addiction, therapy may be helpful for you. Sometimes getting support for ourselves can be the best support for our loved ones who are managing a condition of their own.

Q: How is therapy different than talking to a friend or family member?

I know earlier I gave an intense and off the cuff answer. Here is a more detailed and professional response I'd like to share. To describe this simply- family and friends may tell us what they think, what we should do or what they would do if they were us. A mental health professional skillfully asks questions with purpose and challenges thoughts we may have about ourselves and others. The mental health professional and the client take time to discuss what decisions or choices the person has and may discuss how our relationship with others affects our feelings and choices. A therapist's job is not to tell someone what to do. We invite and guide discussion to ensure our client's reasons for coming in are met with attention to detail, challenging perspective, encouraging growth and exploring change. We educate on symptoms of mental health conditions and prognosis, we provide insight and support to your challenges, life changes, accomplishments and victories. It's really a one-of-a-kind experience. We all deserve time to ourselves to work towards a feel-good more-often-life.

Q: How long can therapy take?

How long therapy takes varies; It can be short or long. This is really a discussion to have with your therapist and will depend on the reason you joined therapy and what you hope to accomplish. It is beneficial to let your therapist know if you have a timeline of your own. This will allow the both of you to discuss the time frame and work to meet your expectations.

What may I want to focus on if I join therapy?

_____

_____

_____

_____

_____

_____

_____

_____

_____

_____

_____

_____

_____

"We got to take care of each other. So if you see somebody that's hurting don't look away. And if you're hurting, even though it might be hard, try to find that bravery within yourself to dive deep and go tell somebody." – Lady Gaga

Heartful #2: How to Support our Loved Ones

Supporting a friend or family member who is experiencing symptoms of a mental health condition can be helpful to both the person with a condition and the supporter as well. Being a support can offer your loved one comfort, strength and stability. Conversely, your loved one may be able to offer insight by sharing their experience and how they have been working to manage their mental health.

How to offer and provide support:

- If you notice someone displays a change in their sleep, appetite, mood and interactions with others this is an indicator to encourage discussion around how someone is feeling. If your friend or family member is showing signs of a mental health concern you can offer support by sharing your concerns and observations, explaining that you are invested in learning about their experience.

- If you have questions you intend to ask it is worthwhile to share why the answers can be helpful to you. Insight gained through your questions can help you better understand what they are going through. If they would like more support or help this could be an opportunity to provide that support.

- If your family or friend is working to manage their

mental health condition you can offer support by asking them to share their experience. You can inquire as to how often they have symptoms, how they are currently managing, and if they are seeking professional support.

- If your loved one is under the care of professional support you could encourage them to share with you the experience they have with their professional support. You may want to ask, "How do you think it is going?" "How often do you get a chance to meet?" and "Would you like anything different?" It is supportive to share that you are interested in learning about their condition such as diagnosis, symptoms, prognosis and treatment options. It is also supportive to ask if they would like you to participate in their appointments every now and then for additional support and education.

- If your loved one is not under the care of professional support perhaps ask if they have considered professional support as an option. If they have, it is worthwhile to discuss why they have not yet sought out support. It is supportive to validate your loved one's concerns and it is supportive to help identify any barriers to your loved one seeking care.

Barriers may include: limited access to the internet, transportation concerns, reading difficulties, or worries about meeting with a professional support. Consider asking if they have access to the internet, or if they need assistance using the internet. Perhaps secure a time to sit down and help them navigate a computer or smartphone. It is also supportive to offer your family or friend assistance in finding a professional support that may be a good fit for them. Think out loud together. Perhaps ask if there is a preference for gender, or if they prefer to work with someone who may be younger or older. Inquire if they have a place in mind already or if there is a location they prefer.

Preparing for a first time visit with a professional support:

- If you have access to the internet, browse for a website and look for information on what you may expect during your initial visit (i.e. expected appointment length, can you fill out paperwork online if you prefer to take care of that ahead of time). Many professionals have websites that provide information about the team members, their specialties and what a newcomer can expect during their visits. One can also call and ask to speak with someone regarding expectations during the first visit.

- If you schedule a first-time appointment and are driving yourself, ask about parking availability. Ask if the office is locked during office lunch hours and if so, what time the doors are re-opened.

- Have a list of questions and concerns you would like your provider to be aware of. You and your provider may discuss some of these questions during this visit or may prepare to discuss further during a future visit. Bring a list of your medical diagnoses and any currently prescribed medication(s). It is important to discuss what your medications are prescribed for as some medications have a dual purpose. It is worthy to note that without proper and on-going evaluation medical conditions can appear to be mental health conditions or vice versa. In addition, it is worthy to note that reactions to drug use can appear as a mental health condition. Choosing to be honest with your treatment provider about your diagnoses and drug use serves a great deal of insight for both short- and long-term care.

- If your professional support shares an observation or shares information that you do not fully understand ask them to provide an example or break down the information in a way that is better understood and relatable.

- After your initial visit, take time to think about what you liked, may wish had been different, and make a list of any questions or thoughts you can discuss during your next visit. If you are feeling unsettled or uncertain about your appointment you can discuss this with your professional support who can offer insight and guidance about your experience. It is necessary and it is invited to discuss any questions or concerns to produce change.

Choosing a support to be involved in your mental health wellness:

It is important to ask ourselves who we feel support from and who we would like to be involved in our mental health care. Having support involved in enhancing our mental well-being can be life changing. But don't forget... people in our lives do not know what we're going through unless they ask or if we tell them ourselves.

"A lot of people undermine their own depression and anxiety. Nothing's necessarily going wrong. It just happens and it's just inside of you and that's not something you should be ashamed of. It's justified because it's happening."
– Lili Reinhart

Heartful #3: Why do some people feel depressed if nothing bad has happened?

Sometimes we know that we're depressed. Sometimes we may be depressed and not be aware of it, but recognize something is "off." And sometimes we know we are depressed but feel we have no good reason to be.

Depression varies in its severity. It is worthwhile to recognize some of the traits of depression. You may be surprised what you learn. Traits of depression may include: down or sad mood, loss of interest in activities you typically enjoy (maybe you like to read, go for walks, or spend time with friends and you no longer make time to enjoy these things). You may notice a change in your sleep, concentration or weight. You may feel easily fatigued or slowed down, have feelings of guilt, feel worthless and/or have thoughts of not wanting to be alive. These are all possible and may be more pronounced during certain times of the year: notable dates, changes in season and daylight savings time.

Equally as important as recognizing the traits of depression is identifying what has caused them to develop over time. And to understand and accept that sometimes the cause is not related to something "bad" that happened. Often it is a combination of factors that influence our mood, not just a life-changing event.

I prefer to think of natural causes versus eventful causes. Eventful causes are the more obvious to identify often connected to a life-altering event such as a loss to death, loss of a job, a relationship that has come to an end, loss of a home, a vehicle accident, violence or events that have caused Post Traumatic Stress Disorder (PTSD). But what actually causes depression if nothing bad has happened? Some may feel they do not have a reason to be depressed due to "success," however one may measure that (i.e. money, a career, they look happy, they're getting married, they go on vacation every year, they "have it all"). Natural causes tend to develop, over time, related to pressure we put on ourselves to reach goals, maintain success, or strive for perfection. Others may pressure us to maintain a certain lifestyle. And probably one of the more relatable pressures is comparison to others (social media anyone?). And last but certainly not least, genetics or chemical changes in the brain (sometimes called a chemical imbalance).

I promise I won't get all "science-y" explaining the biology and neurology components (that's not my area of expertise anyway). But what I will share is that, for some of us, chemistry in our brains can play a role in causing depression. When there is not enough of the "feel good" chemicals in our brain we feel the effects in how we think, feel and behave. And the more we ignore it the worse it can become over time. The takeaway here is that the imbalance of brain chemicals can be improved with a combination of medication and therapy. The medication (prescribed by a doctor or nurse) provides the chemicals while the therapist assists us in identifying the factors that lead to the depletion, while learning how to develop, put into practice, and maintain a healthy mood.

Other factors that may influence the development of depression may be a lack of connection with other people, limited support, and not enough family-time. Having a medical condition or addiction can influence our mood and behavior. Not having time, we need to work towards goals or dreams may cause irritability and feeling helpless. Leaving a job, ending a relationship, or setting boundaries with people in our lives can cause feelings of guilt which is a symptom of depression. Other times, we may fear how others may react if we share that we're depressed such as letting someone down, causing those who may rely on us to worry, perhaps we fear others may not find us reliable or dependable any more, or may blame us for change or for choices we make... that is a TON of pressure. Sometimes we may find ourselves feeling guilty because others "have it worse." Sometimes we may feel depressed because we do not feel we deserve to be depressed. Or we can't "justify it" if we have other things in life we are satisfied about or other people admire us for. Please know, there is no "checklist" to determine who has a right to experience depression. But there is a checklist of who deserves to feel better and have support. That checklist item is: Everyone.

We have to take care of ourselves first. **We cannot be our best for others if we are not our best for ourselves.** If you notice you are experiencing signs of depression, begin looking for a mental health professional for yourself and make an appointment. Also start identifying who you would like to accompany you on your journey of healing and allow them to participate. Remember… people do not know what we are going through unless they ask (and we tell them the truth) or we tell them ourselves.

"I think it's important to have closure in any relationship that ends – from a romantic relationship to a friendship. You should always have a sense of clarity at the end and know why it began and why it ended. You need that in your life to move cleanly into your next phase of life."
– Jennifer Aniston

Heartful #4: BE SELF-ISH when seeking a long-term partner

Have you ever seen the show, The Bachelor or The Bachelorette? I'm not going to lie... my hand is in the air. My viewing of the show started out as curiosity surrounding the fact the show had even been approved to air. Then I did a Google search, finding out it has been on the air since 2002! Anyway, what started out as curiosity transitioned into surprise and concern. I kept asking myself why we didn't see the contestants having real life conversations like:

- Do you want kids?
- Why or why not?
- What is your relationship like with your family?
- Are you spiritual or religious?

Then I reminded myself that we, as the audience, only see an hour of footage each week. The show could just be omitting those conversations. Anywho... it got me thinking.

First, I'd love to be the pre-marital therapist consult for these "dating" couples (Dear ABC- hint, hint) and second, I wanted to develop a list of questions to ask yourself and a potential partner to assist in compatibility for a hopeful, healthier partnership.

Below you will find thoughts and questions to consider when seeking a long-term partner. These topics could be discussed while dating AND throughout your relationship because we DO change.

Communication

- Do you express your thoughts the way you intend to?
- Do you think your friends and family would agree with you?
- Do you have difficulty talking about particular subjects? If so, what are they and what do you experience when these topics are brought up? Is there anyone in your life you feel more comfortable talking with about difficult subjects? If so, what makes you feel more at ease?

Discuss management of frustration and anger. All these discussions are worthwhile.

- Do you raise your voice?
- Do you have a history of physical altercations?
- Do you throw objects or cause harm to yourself or others in the heat of the moment?

Privacy

- Discuss what this means to each of you and what this means to your family members.
- Discuss if you feel you are able to respect one another's privacy and why you may have

challenges doing so.

What makes you uncomfortable?

- Social events, work gatherings, family parties, being alone, certain people?
- Responsibilities, committing to a plan?
- Discussing intimacy, discussing family history, medical or mental health conditions?
- Talking about life changing events you have experienced?

Discuss how each of you handle uncomfortable situations individually and how you could support one another in challenging moments.

Please note, you do not have to discuss details. You can, rather, let your partner know when you need support and how they can support you when difficult times arise.

Support

Describe what support looks and feels like for each of you.

- Give examples of when you have felt supported by someone in your life and think of an example of when you did not feel supported when you expected to be.
- Think about and talk about what kind of support

you want, how and when. Do you expect support in the form of words, forms of affection, or physically being there when needed?
- Consider how support relates to work, mental health, and management of medical conditions.
- What would support sound and feel like for you?
- Maybe you would like to feel support in setting boundaries with family, seizing personal goals, and dedicating more time to enjoying hobbies.
- Share what you like and don't like, want more of and need less of and why this is helpful for you.

Physical, medical and mental health

- Consider your health concerns, medical and mental health conditions and medications you take to support your own health.
- Determine if you want to share your history with your partner. If so, ask yourself why this could be important and decide what you will share.
- Discuss how your partner's support could be helpful in managing any of your conditions. If you are uncertain if you would like to discuss your conditions with your partner consider discussing this with your doctor or a therapist. Your provider may be able to provide insight or peace of mind while in a safe and confidential place to have these conversations.

Attraction

- Discuss what attracts you to others.
- What about their personality do you find appealing?
- Are you attracted to a person who is able to remain calm and reflect patience when under stress?
- Are you drawn to someone who reflects confidence and commitment?
- Do you admire someone's empathy for others, desire to help others, and the way someone expresses themselves?
- Are you attracted to people who exhibit style (from clothing to decorating to friendliness)?
- Do you gravitate toward people eager to try new things?

You may notice you enjoy being around those who have similar interests as you. Maybe this person enjoys nature, or makes time to enjoy hobbies they have. Maybe you are both animal lovers, like to cook, or have interest in traveling. Compatibility is key.

Employment

There's a lot to discuss here. From expectations of one another to expectations of yourself. These questions are intended for each of you to answer.

- Do you work? If not- discuss why including any

challenges, barriers or concerns related to employment.

- If you do work- how would you describe a typical day and week in your job?
- How often do you work?

Discuss what you'd prefer was different in your workplace.

- Do you anticipate or are you working towards a role change that could become more demanding of your time?
- Where in your life are you now, in relation to your career goals?
- It is worthwhile to discuss if work has impacted your relationships with others in your life and how.
- Do you find yourself ever considering how you would balance your time or how to make changes if you want more time with family and friends than your job permits?
- How would you know if you were working more than is desirable?
- And last but not least, how can I or we, as your loved ones, support you in balancing your time?

Regarding your co-workers, discuss:

- Who is a central part of your daily interactions while at work?
- What you enjoy about your workplace and

colleagues.

- Concerns or observations you make about your colleagues and even yourself.
- When someone new has been hired.
- Any concerns you may have about your partner working closely with colleagues.
- How to approach discussing worries, concerns or insecurities your partner may have.

It's sometimes worthwhile to discuss when someone new has been hired. Encourage one another to share concerns you may have about your partner working closely with a colleague(s). Think out loud how you could approach one another if you had worries, or insecurities. Perhaps consider introducing your partner to colleagues you work closely with.

Socialization with friends

- Share what each of you consider to be "socializing."
- Discuss your current socialization.
- Discuss why socialization has OR has not changed over time.
- Discuss if you would like your socialization to increase, decrease or remain the same and discuss why this would be worthwhile.

Family, friends

- Discuss how important friends and family are to

each of you and why they are important.

- Describe to your partner how your closest people in your life bring value to your life and even hardship.
- Discuss how each of you manage difficult relationships within your lives and how you could support one another in managing stress that can develop.

Intimacy

- Consider both physical and emotional intimacy. Identify for yourself what you enjoy, need and expect.
- Consider the type of physical connection and interactions each of you desire including the frequency and type of physical intimacy you expect or hope for.
- Discuss if either of you are uncomfortable or not interested in fulfilling requests or preferences of the other.
- Regarding emotional intimacy, discuss what you enjoy, want more of, and need to feel attractive, loved, wanted, respected, and secure.
- Discuss qualities in a relationship you desire and that you have admired from other relationships you have noticed.
- Discuss thoughts and expectations related to monogamy and non-monogamous relationships.
- If either of you are worried or uncomfortable discussing intimacy with one another consider

talking with a therapist individually, as a unit, or both.

Decision making

Perhaps consider a discussion of how decision making was made in your own life that you saw as a child, as a teen and now portray as an adult. Discuss how each of you would hope to integrate joint decision making and what you would prefer to maintain as your own decision making specifically for yourself (i.e. money, family relationships, bank accounts, purchases, priorities).

Money

Money, money, money, money, money, moooooooneyyy. Okay. So I sang that in my head and wrote it so many times that my brain is playing that trick on me where you're not even sure if you spelled the word correctly anymore and all of a sudden you're second guessing whether or not it's even a word. Literally laughing out loud. I'm now going to google why that happens and if there is a word for it.

I'm baaaaaaack. Technology is quite impressive. I googled "how come when I repeat a word over and over it starts to lose its meaning and you get confused." Welp… it's called Semantic Satiation. Because I suck at all science, I am just going to tell you what I interpret as the cause. When we naturally start talking, our brain automatically begins processing the words in the sentence that were just spoken. If we repeat the word over and over the brain is no longer trying to process a thought because there are no accompanying words to formulate a sentence. So basically, the brain starts to recognize the word by sound, not meaning, because we are repeating it. Because we are not often focused on the sound of the word, that's what the brain is doing in this instance—hearing the word for its sound not its meaning hence, why it is so unfamiliar. They say you learn something new every day.

Pretty F-ing awesome! I love fun facts.

Now, back to money. Consider your thoughts on money.

- Are you a saver?
- Are you a financial worrier?
- Do you spend more than you intend or want to?
- Do you have debt? If so, how are you working to manage debt?
- Do you consider yourself to live within or outside of your means?
- Do you prefer to have separate or joint checking accounts; why or why not?

Talk about how you would hope to discuss finances and financial concerns.

- Who would prefer to be responsible for paying which bills?
- Whose names will be on the bills?
- Would you like to hold each other accountable to staying on track with monthly or annual goals?

Consider financial needs, financial goals, identify what is financially important to you, support one another in willingness to learn more about one another's financial concerns and goals. Consider seeking consult and guidance from a financial planner, if desirable.

Religion, Spirituality, the absence of either, Heritage, Race, Family tradition, Culture

Whether you're committed, undecided, somewhere in between or not affiliated with any religious or spiritual connection it is important to find out where each other falls within this category. Discussions of how our Religion, Heritage, Race, Culture and family traditions can greatly impact our ability to understand and connect with one another. It is important for each partner to share how they experience the world. Having these discussions provides perspective we would otherwise not be aware of about one another. Never assume. Ask. Ask again if you struggle to understand. This allows us to see how values, morals and life experiences impact us individually which in turn can impact the stability, security, respect and love within a relationship.

Housekeeping

Discuss how each of you maintain your own home (i.e. from dishes to cleaning, bathroom hygiene, making the bed, to laundry, to outdoor maintenance, to cooking). This can be eye-opening. Especially if you choose not to live with one another prior to marriage.

Mental health

It is important to consider how one another interprets mental health placement in our lives.

- Do we experience mental health conditions ourselves? Are we comfortable discussing it?
- Were we encouraged by family or friends growing up to discuss mental health, talk about feelings, problems, worries and concerns?
- How are our experiences different from one another?
- Discuss comfortability surrounding discussions of emotions and mental health.
- Ask yourself what you would need from your partner to feel comfortable sharing your mental health experiences.
- Are we able to recognize deficits, changes or concerns in our own mental health well-being?
- Do you take time to learn about mental health wellness?
- What would we want our partners to understand

about our own mental health wellness and the support we hope to receive from one another?

Alcohol and other drug use

Discussion of alcohol and drug history can be beneficial for many reasons. This discussion allows for both parties to be aware if either have hard-set thoughts related to alcohol and drugs. Perhaps one partner is against any use, or one partner has a history of addiction or a family history of addiction. It's worthwhile to discuss how your history may impact your relationship or how, as a unit, you will recognize warning signs, navigate concerns, and be a support. Working with a substance use specialist can assist partners in understanding alcohol and drug use and offer support to both you and your partner.

Where you live, where your family lives and how this relates to where you want to live

- Discuss what you like and dislike about where you live.
- Discuss if either of you have aspirations to relocate or have considered doing so.
- Discuss what holds you back or any barriers to relocating, if you desire to live elsewhere.

How were you treated as a child, teen and young adult

Discuss how your own experience relates to the following:

- Feeling love and affection from guardians (i.e. being told we are loved, receiving physical touch such as hugs).
- The discipline style that was experienced.
- Family dynamics.
- Traditions you had.
- Celebration of holidays, birthdays, and achievements.
- How you experienced support during challenging times, embarrassment and loss.

Discuss your thoughts on having children

- If you do want children- how many and why?
- Do you have any fears or worries being a parent?
- How do you hope to parent? What would this look like to each of you?
- What did you like and not like about your own childhood?
- Do you and your partner align with your ideal parenting including showing love, spending time with one another and discipline styles?
- Think futuristic as well. How will each parent respond to the gender and sexual preference of their child?
- Discuss if you are on the same page and what this means to the both of you.

Consider discussions of preparing for care of a child

- How will having a child impact your career, finances, independence and interactions with family?
- Who would you like to help out and who do you absolutely not want help from (i.e. family or friends?)—that's a serious question that deserves attention.
- How will each partner balance disruption in sleep, late night /early morning feedings, showering, preparing and eating meals?
- Discuss how to recognize if either party needs a break and time to themselves.
- Identify who you will reach out to when you need time to catch up on sleep, shower, take a bath, get out of the house or eat a meal uninterrupted.
- Discuss how to approach one another when you want help or need time to yourself.

Grief

When we hear the word grief we may often relate it to death. I prefer to also think of grief as loss related to anything in life that means something of value to us:

- The loss of a friendship or relationship with a family member due to a disagreement or because we grew apart.
- The loss of a job because we were laid off, or

- fired, or we resigned because it was too much to manage or maybe we just hated it.
- The loss of identity related to retirement.
- The loss experienced from divorce or the ending of a relationship (i.e. familiarity of a home, access to children, access to pets, financial security, loss of our once stable and comfortable relationships with our ex-partner's family and friends).
- The bittersweet loss felt when children grow, become independent and make lives of their own.

Grief is life changing. Our relationship with grief may change over time but we will feel the grief in some capacity indefinitely. Grief can be exacerbated by notable dates and can be unexpected in its arrival, taking our breath away with its slap in the face. It is important to identify who we trust to respect our thoughts, feelings, hardships and needs, and allow them to be a part of our journey.

Grief related to death and how to talk to people we know who lost a loved one: I see and hear this more often than not. If we have a friend, or acquaintance or a co-worker who lost a loved one, some of us do not feel comfortable reaching out to share our condolences. Sometimes people are unsure if they should reach out to someone, and question what to say. Acknowledgment reflects a caring heart. If you struggle with words consider what you would want someone to share with you. Or simply put, let someone know that you care very much about their pain.

Past relationships: Consider what you liked, disliked, and want more of and less of in your next relationship. Consider aspects of other's relationships you have observed that you admire. Consider traits and qualities of people you admire and want within yourself and your future partner.

Odds and ends but equally as important as the others

Discuss thoughts related to:

- Pets
- Exercise habits (or lack of)
- Physical health needs
- Self-esteem
- Dreams
- Goals
- Daily routines
- Sleep patterns
- Do you need naps?
- Alone time preferences
- Hobbies you have
- Sports interest
- Television and movie content, you prefer
- Personal space expectations

The above categories allow conversation around compatibility and support of one another's wants and needs. Through these discussions you will see how and where you two connect, your enthusiasm, and if you support one another's lifestyle preferences.

You have one life on this planet Earth. Remember that.

What are your most important discussion points
with a potential new partner and why?

_____

_____

_____

_____

_____

_____

_____

_____

_____

_____

_____

THE RANDOM STUFF

Webster's definition of Random:

Random—adjective

Collegiate Definition (Entry 2 of 3) 1b: made, done, or chosen at random

Webster's definition of Stuff:

Stuff—noun

Collegiate Definition (Entry 1 of 2) 5c: a matter to be considered

Integrating Peace and Calm Into Your Life: Mindful Activity

Use your five senses to prepare for and to enjoy a present moment:

Eating: Enjoy your food. Think ahead of time about what you are in the mood to eat. Consider planning ahead of time food you want to have in your home, restaurants you may want to treat yourself to, and do not rush eating. Savor the flavor. Enjoy your meal alone or in the company of others.

Taking a shower or bath: Do you prefer the water to be hot, warm or cool? Consider the lighting of the area and make adjustments for enjoyment such as bright, cool, or dim. Think of calming scents whether it be a candle or your favorite scented body wash. Consider sound. Do you prefer quiet or perhaps music? If choosing music, be mindful if you want lyrics or instrumental only. If you prefer lyrics consider the genre of music you prefer for your mood. Music can make us release emotions. Choose wisely when working to wind down and relax.

Sleep: Consider the temperature of the room. Consider the pillow you want to use, the position of your bed, and the lighting you prefer in your resting state. Consider noise. Do you need silence or do you prefer to have background noise of the television or music?

Making important phone calls: When making important phone calls set aside a time that you can commit to that day. Decide where you want to make the phone call (which room in your home, a quiet place with little distraction and noise). Have all of your important information laid out in front of you. Have a list of questions or needs you hope to discuss during the phone call. Have a pen and paper available to make notes.

Reminders for Long-Term Self-Care

- Schedule and attend an annual physical exam with your primary care doctor.
- Ask your doctor or specialist what your diagnoses, conditions, symptoms and treatment options are.
- If you do not understand advice or suggestions provided by the doctor ask them to clarify or give examples.
- If you choose not to follow the recommendations of your provider (i.e. taking medications, completing lab work, attending appointments) please inform your doctor. The doctor may discuss alternate options or see you more often to monitor your condition(s).
- Schedule and attend, minimally, two teeth cleanings a year. Even if you hate doing it you will hate it less than if you have to go because you're in unbearable pain as a result of putting off maintenance visits.
- Consider physical health related to food and water: Consider making a priority of enjoying meals during the day and drinking the classic 8 glasses of water a day to enhance a healthy colon or gut health. Your food lifestyle and preferences are worth discussing with your doctor. Your doctor can consult your medical records and provide recommendations that can enhance gut health. Consult with your doctor if you have any bathroom habits you desire to be different or are

uncertain if they should be different.

- Some medication side effects can impact bathroom habits that are worth discussing with your prescriber. Your prescriber can provide suggestions and may be able to make an adjustment if desirable. And last but not least, if able, move your body. Enjoy a walk, engage in some form of exercise. Even stretching and dancing counts. Crank the music for goodness sake!

- Identify any loved ones you may want aware of your conditions and invite them to learn more.

- Consider the effects of alcohol and other drug use: Alcohol and other drugs impact our mood, how we take care of ourselves, how we interact with others and can also disrupt the body's natural desire to eat. Additionally, mental health symptoms can be exacerbated with alcohol and other drug use. If you have any questions or concerns related to substance use for yourself or loved ones there are professionals of substance use and mental health specialty who share education, guidance and support. If the internet is accessible, one can research providers in the area desired, one can contact their doctor's office for referrals, or one can consult with their health insurance company for professionals accepting new patients.

- Make time to spend with people you enjoy being around and make you feel comfortable.

- Make time for alone time.

- If you have a partner in your life make time for a 'date night.'
- Make time to enjoy activities and hobbies (see the activity list at the end of this book).
- **MAKE TIME TO DO MORE OF WHAT YOU LOVE!**

What are your current health care goals?

_____

_____

_____

_____

_____

_____

_____

_____

_____

_____

_____

_____

What are your long-term health care goals?

_____

_____

_____

_____

_____

_____

_____

_____

_____

_____

_____

_____

Webster definition of Bucket list:

Bucket list—noun

Collegiate definition: a list of things that one has not done before but wants to do before dying

If you've never considered having a bucket list before, now is the time.

Having a list of things you want to try, places you want to see, and events you want to attend gives us moments to look forward to. Having a bucket list gives us time to prepare and work towards check-marking those dreams into grand memories.

Experiencing bucket list items impacts our energy and our mood, while promoting livelihood, ambition, fulfillment and satisfaction.

Nothing is too small and nothing is too big. All categories acceptable.

What are your Bucket List items to experience in your City?

_____

_____

_____

_____

_____

_____

_____

_____

_____

_____

_____

_____

What are your Bucket List items to experience in your State?

_____

_____

_____

_____

_____

_____

_____

_____

_____

_____

_____

_____

_____

What are your Bucket List items to experience in your Country?

_____

_____

_____

_____

_____

_____

_____

_____

_____

_____

_____

_____

_____

What are your Bucket List items to experience in another Country?

_____

_____

_____

_____

_____

_____

_____

_____

_____

_____

_____

_____

_____

Generating Passion In Our Children: To Feel Good, To Experience Meaning, Develop Purpose And Have A More Peaceful Life

When you ask a kid what they want to be when they grow up, they either tell you exactly what they want to be or they have no idea. Sometimes kids go off to college and have no idea what they are going to do. I've thought about this for a long time.

Let's start young. Elementary school. Let's start integrating weekly field trips to different businesses and job sites where children can organically develop and gravitate towards an interest that is driven by curiosity and passion.

Take field trips to:

- Construction sites, airports, architect's offices, car manufactures, mechanic shops
- Restaurants, hotels
- Hospitals, different type of doctor's offices (chiropractic, neurology, dermatology, veterinarian)
- Museums, garden centers, a zoo and aquarium
- Fashion institutes, television studios, News studios
- Plays, musical theater, exposure to musical instruments, radio stations
- Salons of hair and nail services, spas of massage and relaxation

- Expose children to public speakers, authors, writing
- Fitness gyms with personal trainers
- Marketing and advertising, newspaper / print companies
- Criminal justice jobs such as touring a police academy, police station, court rooms, a fire hall
- Tour water waste facilities, recycling and garbage facilities

The opportunities for exposure to different jobs is endless. Those are just a handful in the ever-growing world. Children will naturally gravitate toward an area of interest. Through interest develops curiosity, ideas, creativity, vision, passion and motivation. Can you imagine how different the world could be if we develop a passion before the world gets its hands on us? Before societal, social media, peer and family pressure influences and dictates our choices?

Rather than trying to obtain higher test scores why don't we instead channel our energy on igniting and supporting organic passion in our children which in turn may produce an increase in test scores- or not. Some kids hate school. Feeling not good enough, not smart enough, judged for poor grades, perhaps feeling that others may not think they will succeed. For some students, a field trip is the only time they may look forward to school. Through field trips their energy is focused on observing and learning in a visual and physical sense.

The takeaway message here is that not all children are loved by their guardians, not all children grow in a safe and encouraging home environment, not all children are made to think or believe they can do anything they set their mind to. The earlier we can have children develop an innate passion can result in developing SELF-WORTH, motivation, independence, dedication, creativity, commitment, fulfillment, satisfaction, contribution, meaning, purpose, and self-love which can lead to peace.

If your education system does not integrate this you, as a guardian, can work to develop local clubs and partner with sponsors who support igniting passion and worth in our world's children.

That's my two cents. Thank you for listening.

College Versus No College

A college degree is not needed to do well in life. College is needed if your dream job requires a degree or certification or license.

Below you will find two topics 1) Narrowing down the type of job you might want and 2) How to go about deciding if the job is right for you. By deciding the type of job you want you can then determine if college would be a necessity.

Narrowing down the type of job you might want: The key is defining the type of business you hope to work for, how you want to be involved in your work place, and the responsibilities you hope to have.

When considering the type of business, you hope to be a part of think about the following:

- Do I prefer to work in a large company with many coworkers or a small company?
- The type of people I prefer or do not prefer to interact with in the workplace (children, young adults, elderly, or having no preference).
- Would I prefer to work with a team on a daily basis to meet goals and expectations or working independently throughout the day?
- Would I like to work with a company that has face to face interactions with customers and clients or telephonically?

- Is there a company I admire and would like to be a part of?

Consider narrowing down areas of interest for your future career. Below are a handful of examples of different career paths:

- Physical health (physical therapist, physical education teacher, fitness instructor)
- Teaching (students or working as a trainer within a company)
- Science and mathematics through technology, architecture, engineering (working in a school, college, or for a dream company you have in mind)
- Electricity, plumbing, waste management
- Writing, art, music, theater, film
- Working with animals
- Guidance counselor, career counselor
- Public speaking (broadcasting through radio or reporting television news)
- Hospitality (hotel management, restaurants)
- Skin care (dermatology or cosmetic/medical such as an esthetician)
- Spa (massage, skin, hair, nails)
- Accounting (managing individual persons or companies' finances)
- Financial planning (helping people manage money as they work towards their retirement and manage finances after retirement)
- Medical field (working as a doctor or nurse,

medical equipment specialist, or rather interested working a non-medical position within a doctor's office or hospital)
- Medicine (pharmaceuticals, pharmacist)
- Mental health, psychology, social work, substance use treatment
- Researcher (data collection and reporting)
- Criminal justice (law enforcement, police officer, probation officer, criminal investigator)
- Coroner or working for a funeral home
- Human Resources (finding candidates to interview for the workplace, handling conflicts in the work place, providing trainings to the workplace regarding compliance rules, issues and concerns)
- Marketing/advertising

There are so many jobs within jobs themselves. Once you can narrow down what type of setting you may want to work in you can also consider the type of job you might enjoy most.

How to go about deciding if the job is right for you:

If there's a job you're interested in, ask if you can talk with someone who is doing the job you might want.

Ask them:

- What are the criteria needed to meet the job requirements?

- What was the process to getting the position?
- What is your experience and how has the job changed over time?
- Is the job what you thought it was going to be?
- What do you like and not like?
- Is there anything you wish you knew about the job before coming into this field?

My motto is you got nothing to lose by asking.

That's my two cents. Thank you for listening.

What are your interests you would like to learn more about?

_____

_____

_____

_____

_____

_____

_____

_____

_____

_____

_____

_____

If Applying For A Job And Attending An Interview

Preparing to apply for the job:

- First things first; learn as much as you can about the company. Check to see if the company you're applying to has a website. If they do, take your time and review it.
- If there's a website check out the Team Members and read their bios; read the mission statement of the company; read the About section that shares where the company came from, how they got to where they are and where they want to go in their future.
- Read about the services that are provided by the company and learn about services you are not familiar with. Ask friends if they know anyone who works for the company of interest and see if you can talk with them about the company.
- If you apply and are waiting for a response and not getting one within the timeframe you were expecting, you can call or email to inquire when an applicant will hear if they are chosen for an interview or not.

If you apply and receive an interview please note the following:

You got an interview scheduled because 1) you meet the required qualifications and 2) they are interested in you.

When you get there, interview THEM.

They are already interested in you. You do not need to sell yourself (unless they ask you to come back for a follow up interview—then sell away).

Questions to consider asking during the interview:

- Is this a new role? If not, how long has the company had this position? What is the expected learning curve based on others' performance in this role?
- What are the challenges others in this role have experienced and what support have they received to enhance their performance and success?
- What does a typical day and week look like for this role?
- What are the strengths you are seeking in a candidate for this position?
- Has the position changed over time and is it expected to change in the coming years?
- What do your employees share they enjoy most about working here?
- What is the starting salary, what are the benefits (i.e. is there time off, sick time, how are these accrued? Is there a company appreciation day?)

Make sure you have identified your own strengths and weaknesses.

If you are having a difficult time ask others how they would describe your attributes.

Strengths to consider:

- Reliable (on time to work, give advance notice for time off request, maybe you have a strong history of being employed at the same job for several years).
- Consider if you have a history of being a team player (offering to assist others who need help or are out on leave). Perhaps you offer suggestions and feedback or maybe you invite suggestions and feedback about your own performance -with confidence and commitment to grow.
- Perhaps you do additional reading or take classes on the side to keep up on information and advancements related to your field.

Weaknesses to consider (it is worthwhile to back up a weakness with a positive action you already have in place to improve):

- Being a perfectionist (although this could actually be a strength for the company). Being a perfectionist reflects your attention to detail and commitment to honoring your work duties however, this can be exhausting. You can relate this weakness to a positive, sharing that you communicate with your boss to ensure work goals are met with balance. But don't forget, you're human which is an acknowledgement that no one is perfect.

- Additional weaknesses may include being 'too nice' or 'forgiving.' You can turn this into a positive by sharing over time you have recognized and put into practice setting professional boundaries. Professional boundaries offer support to ourselves and colleagues. Recognizing if someone needs help you can in turn offer support and guidance to those who may need it.

Having strengths and weaknesses are expected. We all have them. Acknowledge and remind yourself, a weakness you have is someone else's strength just as your strength is someone else's weakness. That is why working together promotes cohesion, advancement, support, long-term growth and satisfaction. Support one another.

That's my two cents. Thank you for listening.

What are your strengths?

_____

_____

_____

_____

_____

_____

_____

_____

_____

_____

_____

_____

What are your weaknesses?

_____

_____

_____

_____

_____

_____

_____

_____

_____

_____

_____

_____

What are questions you would like to ask at your next job interview?

_____

_____

_____

_____

_____

_____

_____

_____

_____

_____

_____

Activity List

Take a class or learn something new like:

- Join a 'Do it yourself' (DIY) group
- Cooking/baking
- Jewelry making
- Sewing
- Birdwatching
- Photography
- Carpentry (contact hardware stores)
- Yoga/Exercise/Dance

Spend time enjoying:

- Museums
- Coffee Shops
- Zoos
- Aquariums
- Pet stores
- Libraries or bookstores
- Historical cemetery or a park
- Bodies of Water (Lake, river, ocean)

Get creative:

- Plant a garden
- Research different topics
- Surprise a family member and take them somewhere special they have been wanting to go
- Volunteer at a place you enjoy or want to learn

more about
- Try a different exercise routine

Maybe you want to:

- Decorate or change the décor in one of your rooms
- Make time to organize closet space
- Get a pet or learn about different pets
- Work on completing a puzzle

Consider:

- Reminisce with friends and family. Happiness and laughter is good for the soul.
- Learning about your ancestry and conducting some research
- Starting a game night
- Making time to watch a movie or start a new television series you're interested in
- Learning fun facts about an area of interest or a person you admire
- Stargazing

Having activities to look forward to allows us to feel productive, motivated and fulfilled. Make time for them.

What are activities you would like to incorporate in to your life?

_____

_____

_____

_____

_____

_____

_____

_____

_____

_____

_____

_____

In closing

Webster definition of closing:

Closing—noun: a concluding part (as of a speech)

Making time to do things you enjoy and are interested in (even alone-embrace it) is what promotes a feel-good-more-often kind of life. A life that everyone deserves.

Remember, we can't be our best for others if we are not our best for ourselves.

I hope you enjoyed this book that represents embracing the self with self-care, self-love, self-compassion, and SELF-ISH decisions.

After all, didn't you hear? Self-ish is the new Selfless.

ABOUT THE AUTHOR

Brittany is a mental health professional whose focus is enhancing well-being by guiding others to do more of what they love without feeling the guilt. Brittany enjoys speaking about the benefits of promoting well-being and enhancing mental health on the daily (in her professional work, on podcasts and television, and in her personal life).

*Fun fact: Brittany's friends and family often refer to her as 'Bee' because she can be sweet as honey but her honesty leaves people feeling her sting. You can often see her wearing a 'Bee' brooch on her sweater as an homage to her nickname.

ACKNOWLEDGEMENTS

To Kathy: You didn't know this… but our first conversation gave me a one-of-a-kind support I haven't felt since my grandmother's passing. I am remarkably grateful.

A special thank you to my grandmother who is no longer with us. Her simplistic memorable phrase has guided my life since I was a child… "Treat others as you wish to be treated little one."

Made in the USA
Monee, IL
25 April 2023